Biff was looking at a book. The book
was about pirates.
"I don't like pirates," she said.

Wilf and Wilma came to play. They
went to Biff's room.

They looked at the little house.
"It's a magic house," said Biff.
"Don't be silly," said Wilma.

They looked at the key.
"It's a magic key," said Chip.
"Don't be silly," said Wilf.

The key began to glow. The magic
was working.
"Oh help!" said Wilma.

The magic was working. The children got smaller and smaller and smaller.

"Oh no!" said Wilf.
"Oh help!" said Wilma.
"We don't like this," they said.

They looked at the house. The windows were glowing. Biff went to the door.

She put the key in the lock. She
opened the door.

The children went inside the house.
"It's a magic house," they said.

"Look at the sand," said Biff.
"Look at the sea," said Chip.
"Come on," they said.

They ran to the sea. Wilf picked up a
shell. Chip picked up a coconut.

Biff climbed up a tree. Wilma went in
the sea.
"This is magic," they said.

They played on the sand. They played
in the sea.
"What an adventure!" said Biff.

A pirate came up. He looked at
the children.
"Children!" said the pirate.

"Pirates!" said the children.
"Oh help!" they said.
"Come on," said the pirates.

The pirates had a boat. They went to
the pirate ship.
"I don't like pirates," said Biff.

"Look at that pirate," said Biff.
"Look at that big rope," said Chip.
"I'm frightened," said Wilf.

"We wanted a party," said the
pirate. "Nobody wanted to come.
Will you come to the party?"

The children went to the party.
It was a good party.
"I like pirates," said Biff.

The key was glowing. It was time
to go.

"Goodbye," said Chip. "Thank you for
the party."
"Oh no!" said the pirates.

"What an adventure!" said Wilma.
"I liked the pirates," said Biff.
Wilf looked at the little hat.